WORLD ALMANAC® LIBRARY
OF THE
AMERICAN REVOLUTION

The Causes
of the American Revolution

Dale Anderson

 WORLD ALMANAC® LIBRARY

Please visit our web site at: www.worldalmanaclibrary.com
For a free color catalog describing World Almanac® Library's list of high-quality books
and multimedia programs, call 1-800-848-2928 (USA) or 1-800-387-3178 (Canada).
World Almanac® Library's fax: (414) 332-3567.

Library of Congress Cataloging-in-Publication Data

Anderson, Dale, 1953-
 The causes of the American Revolution / by Dale Anderson.
   p. cm. — (World Almanac Library of the American Revolution)
 Includes bibliographical references and index.
 ISBN 0-8368-5925-1 (lib. bdg.)
 ISBN 0-8368-5934-0 (softcover)
 1. United States—History—Revolution, 1775-1783—Causes—Juvenile literature.
 I. Title. II. Series.
 E210.A518 2005
 973.3'11—dc22   2005040782

First published in 2006 by
World Almanac® Library
A Member of the WRC Media Family of Companies
330 West Olive Street, Suite 100
Milwaukee, WI 53212 USA

Produced by Discovery Books
Editor: Sabrina Crewe
Designer and page production: Sabine Beaupré
Photo researcher: Sabrina Crewe
Maps and diagrams: Stefan Chabluk
Consultant: Andrew Frank, Assistant Professor of History, Florida Atlantic University
World Almanac® Library editorial direction: Mark J. Sachner
World Almanac® Library editor: Alan Wachtel
World Almanac® Library art direction: Tammy West
World Almanac® Library production: Jessica Morris

Photo credits: American Antiquarian Society: p. 16; CORBIS: pp. 7, 9, 17, 20, 29, 43; Independence National Historical Park:
title page; Library of Congress: pp. 12, 30, 31, 33, 38, 39; National Park Service: p. 34; North Wind Picture Archives: cover, pp. 5,
13, 14, 21, 23, 25, 27, 32, 37, 40, 42.

Printed in Canada

1 2 3 4 5 6 7 8 9 09 08 07 06 05

*Front cover: In December 1773, British colonists in Boston, Massachusetts, threw cases of tea into Boston Harbor in
protest at taxes imposed by the British government. The "Boston Tea Party" was one of many events that led to the
American Revolution.*

*Title page: James Peale painted this portrait of George Washington on horseback in about 1790. He based the
portrait on a work by his brother, Charles Willson Peale—the faces of both the brothers can be seen on the left,
behind Washington. In the background on the right are Revolutionary soldiers, one carrying a French flag.*

Contents

In 1776, the thirteen British **colonies** along the eastern coast of North America declared themselves independent of Britain. The colonists were already fighting British soldiers in protest at British policies. In 1781, the British surrendered to American forces, and, in 1783, they formally recognized the colonies' independence.

A New Nation

The movement from colonies to independence, known as the American Revolution, gave birth to a new nation—the United States of America. Eventually, the nation stretched to the Pacific Ocean and grew to comprise fifty states. Over time, it was transformed from a nation of farmers into an industrial and technological giant, the world's richest and most powerful country.

An Inspiration to Others

The American Revolution was based on a revolution of ideas. The people who led the American Revolution believed that the purpose of government was to serve the people, not the reverse. They rejected rule by **monarchs** and created in its place a **republic**. The founders of the republic later wrote a **constitution** that set up this form of government and guaranteed people's basic rights, including the right to speak their minds and the freedom to worship as they wished.

The ideals on which the United States of America was founded have inspired people all around the world ever since. Within a few years of the American Revolution, the people of France had risen up against their monarchy. Over time, the people of colonies in Central and South America, in Asia, and in Africa followed the U.S. example

*One of the actions taken by the British government that most outraged the colonists was the introduction of the Stamp Act, which placed **taxes** on the goods that colonists bought. In this picture, colonists in Boston take to the street to protest the law.*

and rebelled against their position as colonists. Many former colonies have become independent nations.

The Roots of Revolution

Why did the colonists revolt? After all, in 1750, the vast majority of colonists were proud to be British subjects and content to be part of the British **Empire**. What changed their minds?

The roots of the Revolution can be found in several causes:

- The separation of the colonists from British culture created a distinct American character.
- The colonies and Britain had different **economic** interests.
- Many leading colonists believed in **Enlightenment** ideas of personal rights and liberties.

- Both sides took steps that outraged the other, and these actions brought the two sides to war.

To see how these factors shaped events, it is necessary first to understand the situation in Britain and the American colonies in the 1750s.

The Origins of the Revolution

"What do we mean by the Revolution? The war? That was no part of the Revolution; it was only an effect and consequence of it. The Revolution was in the minds of the people, and this was effected, from 1760 to 1775, . . . before a drop of blood was shed at Lexington."

Revolutionary leader John Adams, letter to Thomas Jefferson, 1815

CHAPTER ONE

Britain and Its Empire

In 1750, Britain was one of the two chief powers in Europe. Spain, although still master of a mighty overseas empire, had fallen on hard times. The Netherlands, which had commanded a profitable empire based on trade in the 1600s, had also declined. Only France rivaled Britain. And a mighty rival it was, with more people and more wealth. Still, Britain had advantages: its navy was the largest in the world, and its economy was thriving.

The British Isles

The island of Great Britain comprises England, Scotland, and Wales. The nation of Britain—today called the United Kingdom of Great Britain and Northern Ireland—includes outlying islands and the northeastern part of Ireland. (In 1750, Britain ruled all of Ireland.)

British Society

In 1750, British society had several layers. At the top was the monarchy, which consisted of the king and his family. Next was the aristocracy, the families with inherited wealth and power. Most were large landowners and held titles, such as duke, marquess, earl, or baronet. This group owned much of the land in Britain and led British society and politics. Next came the middle class, which was growing. This group included professionals such as doctors and lawyers, people who worked in banking and government, and shopkeepers and crafts workers. At the bottom were the poor, who were perhaps 40 percent of the population.

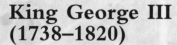

King George III (1738–1820)

At the age of twelve, due to the death of his father, George III became heir to the throne of his grand-father, George II. Ten years later, when his grandfather died, George III became king. He married in 1761 and had fifteen children.

As king, George III wanted to restore the power of the monarch and took much stronger control over the government than his predecessors. In 1765, however, he began to fall victim to porphyria, a disease that caused him severe pain and occasional bouts of insanity.

A strong believer in duty and obedience, George III was determined to make American colonists submit to his will. It was only with great reluctance that he accepted American independence after many years of war. George III's power over the British government declined after the American Revolution, and his insanity increased. In 1811, his son took over George III's duties as king.

Taxes for All

"No one is exempted in this country from paying certain taxes because he is a nobleman or a priest. . . . When the Bill . . . is signed by the king, then the whole nation pays, every man in proportion to his revenue or estate."

French writer and philosopher Voltaire, "Letters on the English," 1778

The British Government

The ruling king or queen had to work closely with Parliament, the British **legislature**. Parliament had two houses. The nobles sat in the House of Lords, while elected representatives of the people filled the House of Commons. The king named members of Parliament as ministers to lead different departments. The prime minister headed the government.

British government was guided by the nation's constitution. This collection of documents and traditional practices defined the limits on government power and the rights of each person.

Life for the Poor

In practice, however, the constitution did little to guarantee quality of life for the poor in Britain. Laborers, servants, and small farmers had almost no prospect of owning their own homes or land. Poor people in the country lived as tenants of the rich landowners and usually worked for them. Poor people in cities often lived in slum conditions or servant quarters.

In addition, the nation was undergoing some changes in the mid-1700s. New farming techniques produced higher crop yields and more food than in the past, but those changes disrupted long-established patterns of living. Farmers and farm laborers were forced off the land. Many flocked to British cities, hoping to find work. There, they found miserable conditions, overcrowding, and poverty. It was these living conditions and lack of future prospects that drove many people to consider a new life in the British colonies in North America.

A Growing Empire

Britain had a growing empire made up of several colonies, the most populated being in North America. The empire also comprised the islands of the West Indies, including Anguilla, Barbuda, and Barbados, which produced sugar. In addition, the British had small colonies on the coast of Central America and at the foot of Africa. They also controlled two ports in India: Bombay and Calcutta.

Britain's goal in having these colonies was to gain wealth. Colonies supplied valuable raw materials and products to the home country, creating income for British businesses. Colonists were good customers for British manufactured goods, too.

Governing the Colonies

In the 1600s and the first half of the 1700s, the British government largely left its colonies in mainland North America alone. This policy, known as "salutary neglect," meant that as long as everything functioned well, the colonists could govern themselves with regard to domestic affairs.

British rulers did appoint royal governors to run the colonies, but colonists also had their own assemblies with lawmakers elected from among their community leaders. This self-government contributed to the spirit of independence found among the colonists. Throughout the 1700s—even well before the turmoil that led to the Revolution—royal governors and colonial assemblies clashed many times. This happened particularly if governors opposed laws proposed by the assemblies or tried to control certain activities, such as **smuggling**.

Settlers in the British colonies of North America were British subjects and, in theory, had constitutional rights. The colonists, however, had no elected representatives in Parliament to speak on their behalf. This issue would become one cause of rebellion.

This engraving shows an English farm and farming equipment in about 1750. Most people who farmed the land worked for rich landowners and had no opportunity to own their own land.

CHAPTER TWO

The Colonies

The British colonies in North America stretched along the Atlantic coast from present-day Maine to Georgia. They can be grouped into three regions—the New England colonies, the middle colonies of the central region, and the southern colonies. The colonies within those regions shared similar geography, resources, economies, and societies.

Although the three regions differed from each other, their residents had in common their independence and a sense of their rights. This fact set them apart from other British subjects and would one day unite the colonies in a revolution.

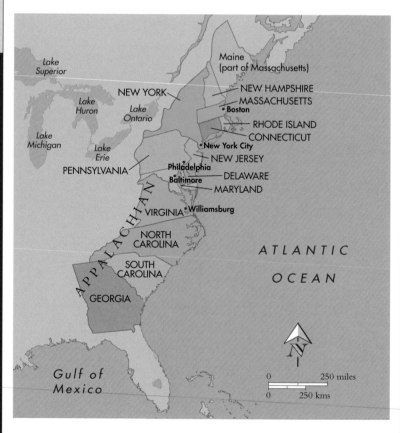

This map shows the thirteen British colonies along the eastern coast of North America in the mid-1700s.

The New England Colonies

The New England colonies—New Hampshire, Massachusetts, Rhode Island, and Connecticut—were settled originally by people who came to North America in the 1600s so they could practice their own religions. Most were **Puritans**, who were treated harshly in England. Puritans settled first in Massachusetts. Rhode Island and Connecticut were founded later by ministers who disagreed with the way the Puritans ran Massachusetts and decided to create new colonies. By the mid–1700s, Puritans were just a minority of New Englanders.

The New England colonies had poor, rocky soil and harsh winters. They were not great places for farming. Most of the population of New England did live on farms, but they were small family establishments, raising just enough food to feed their families and little more.

New England Economy and Government

These colonies had excellent harbors, however, which encouraged shipbuilding, fishing, and overseas trade. The prosperity of these industries helped promote the growth of Boston, one of the colonies' largest cities.

The colonies' leading citizens came from the ranks of successful business owners, lawyers, and ministers. Each New England town had its own government, run by its own people—

The New England Town

New England towns were formed around an open area known as the common or green. This public space was available for recreation and for civic purposes. Commons survive today in cities such as Boston and in many New England towns. Soaring above the common was the town's Puritan church. There, the people gathered on Sunday for long religious services. There, too, town meetings were held, since the church was the largest public space in town.

In the 1700s, Salem, Massachusetts, was a small village typical of New England. People depended on fishing for their living, and the harbor was the center of activity.

at least by those who were male and owned property. The local government met each year in town meetings to make decisions on issues facing the town. These meetings decided what taxes would be paid and how they would be used within the community.

The Middle Colonies

In New England, most white settlers came from the British Isles or were descended from British settlers. The middle colonies (New York, New Jersey, Pennsylvania, and Delaware), however, had sizeable populations from other European countries. More than 15 percent of white settlers in New York and New Jersey had Dutch heritage. About one-tenth of those in Delaware were Swedish. One-third of Pennsylvanians came from Germany.

There was also more religious diversity in these colonies than in New England. Pennsylvania, for instance, had been founded by **Quakers** but was home to many other religions, too.

Fertile soil and a longer growing season made the farms in the middle

Religious Diversity

"We find [in Pennsylvania] Lutherans, Reformed, Catholics, Quakers, Menninists or Anabaptists, Herrnhuter or Moravian Brethren, Pietists, Seventh Day Baptists, Dunkers, Presbyterians, Newborn, Freemasons, Separatists, Freethinkers, Jews, Mohammedans, Pagans, Negroes, and Indians. . . . In one house and one family four, five, and even six sects may be found."

German school teacher Gottlieb Mittelberger, Journey to Pennsylvania, *1750*

Benjamin Franklin (1706–1790)

The most famous and celebrated American of the 1700s—until George Washington gained fame in the Revolution—Benjamin Franklin was a man of many talents. In 1723, Franklin left his native Boston for Philadelphia, where he became a successful printer. He amassed enough of a fortune that he could retire and devote himself to public service.

Franklin was much more accomplished than his business success alone would show. A witty and clever writer, he wrote and published a yearly bestseller in colonial America, *Poor Richard's Almanac*. Possessed of great curiosity, Franklin also discovered some of the basic principles of electricity and gained fame among European scientists as a result. He was the inventor of the lightning rod, bifocal glasses, and an efficient wood stove. Among many other public activities, Franklin ran the colonial postal system and helped found the college that is today the University of Pennsylvania.

Franklin was immensely influential in politics. He played a major role in winning independence, first by sitting in the **Congress**, but more importantly through his work overseas that won a crucial alliance with France. In his eighties, Franklin came out of retirement to take part in the convention that wrote the U.S. Constitution.

Benjamin Franklin (right) at his printing press.

Slave owners in the South visit the slave quarters on their plantation. Slaves were owned, like animals, and worked for no pay.

colonies far more productive than those in New England. Because of this, farmers could produce large crops of wheat and other foods, which they shipped to Europe. The middle colonies carried on a thriving trade from major ports such as New York and Philadelphia.

The Southern Colonies

The southern colonies—Virginia, Maryland, North Carolina, South Carolina, and Georgia—had fewer large cities than the colonies farther north. There were also fewer merchants. In the South, **cash crops** were the focus of the economy. Farmers in Maryland and Virginia grew tobacco and wheat. Those in South Carolina grew rice, sugar, and indigo (a plant producing a valuable blue dye).

The farming system was different from that farther north. Although many farmers worked their own small farms, southern colonies also had large plantations, where enslaved people did the farm labor. The slaves had been brought from Africa against their will and sold at auction to the highest bidder. Slavery was not unique to the South; the other colonies had slavery as well. In the South, however, it was a crucial part of the economy and society, and plantation owners dominated society and politics.

Blacks made up 20 percent or more of the population in the South. In South Carolina, a majority of the people were black. Whites—rich and poor alike—always feared a slave rebellion. When revolts did take place, they were fiercely suppressed.

The Slave Trade

In the 1700s, slaves were treated as goods rather than people, and they were part of an international exchange of goods, or trade. Merchants in New England sent ships carrying rum and iron goods to West Africa. They sold those cargoes and took on board Africans who had been sold into slavery. The merchants brought the slaves across the Atlantic to be sold in the West Indies. There, New Englanders could buy sugar and molasses to take home. This triangular trade, shown below, was just one part of the complex trade routes that flourished between North America, Europe, and Africa in the 1700s.

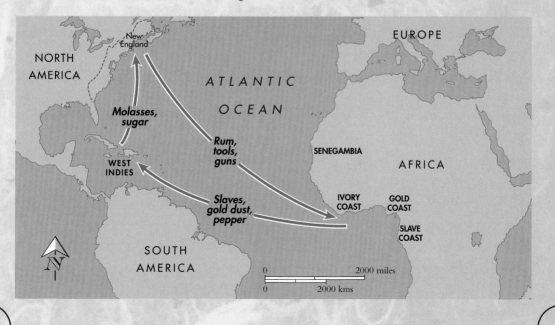

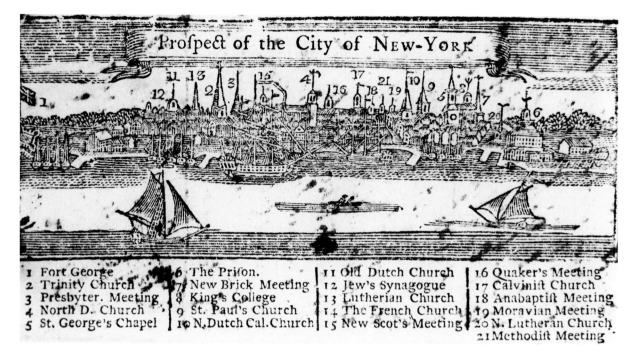

Religion was important in the thirteen colonies of the 1700s. This woodcut of New York City in 1771 marks a large number of churches of varying denominations.

Common Ground

While each region was distinct, the thirteen British colonies shared some traits. Whites formed the majority of the population, more markedly so north of Maryland. Most whites came from Britain and mistrusted people from other groups. Even Benjamin Franklin showed contempt for the Germans streaming into Pennsylvania.

Most Americans were Christians, although there were small communities of Jews in some port cities. Apart from a large Catholic community in Maryland, the vast majority of Christians belonged to Protestant churches and held a deep suspicion of Catholics and other religious groups.

The American colonists also shared certain values. They had a strong belief in their personal rights and liberties and a determination to defend them. Many white colonists owned property or hoped to in the future. This opportunity gave them a feeling of equal status with any other person. There were certainly great differences in wealth, learning, and social standing, but the poorest landholder was still just that—a landholder. If a rich planter visited the house of poor people and abused their hospitality, he could be asked to leave. This was a huge change from Britain, where the poor rarely owned the land they farmed or the homes they lived in.

Fond of Freedom

"The people of this province . . . are chiefly industrious farmers, [craftspeople] or men in trade; they enjoy and are fond of freedom, and the meanest among them thinks he has a right to civility from the greatest."

Pennsylvania Journal, *1756*

Self-Government

Colonists in North America had, for many years, enjoyed the chance to govern themselves. This was not only due to such traditions as the town meeting. Each colony also had its own representative legislature, or colonial assembly, that made laws for the people of that colony. From early on, the colonists were determined not to lose the right to self-rule. Many years after the Revolution, a veteran told an interviewer why he had fought. He said, "We always had governed ourselves and we always meant to. They [the British government] didn't mean we should."

Growth of the Colonies

In the mid–1700s, immigrants continued to arrive, and existing colonists kept producing children. As a result, the population was booming. About 250,000 people lived in the colonies in 1700. By 1750, there were about 1.17 million—an increase of nearly five times. Cities were expanding, settlements were spreading westward, and trade was increasing. There was a feeling of opportunity and growth in the colonies.

The first colonial legislature in the British colonies in North America was the House of Burgesses of Virginia, established in Jamestown in 1619. In 1698, Williamsburg became the capital of the colony, and the House of Burgesses met at this site in Williamsburg from 1704. This building, built in the 1930s, is a reconstruction of the one completed in 1704.

17

CHAPTER THREE

The French and Indian War

In the 1750s, the thirteen British colonies in North America became involved in a conflict called the French and Indian War. The war ended in a British victory over France that was celebrated by the colonists. The conflict, however, had consequences that helped move the colonies toward revolution. It caused leaders from the separate colonies to consider uniting for the first time. And the cost of the war and its aftermath led to a clash between Britain and its colonists.

Rival Powers

In the mid–1700s, the British held the Atlantic coast and northern Canada, but other European

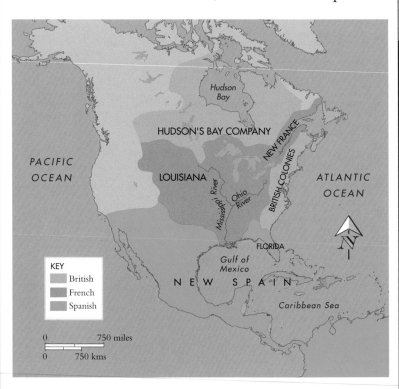

The colony of New France and French-claimed Louisiana held back the British colonies along the coast. But the growing population of British colonists wanted to expand into French territories.

The Albany Plan of Union

The plan Benjamin Franklin presented at Albany called for a union led by a president and a council with members from each colony. Those members would be named by the colonial assemblies. One example Franklin used to support his plan was the successful union of several Native American tribes in the Iroquois Confederacy. This ancient union of five tribes allowed for each group to maintain its own identity, but the whole could unite for common defense when necessary. Franklin proposed that the colonies form a similar union.

powers had colonies in North America. Spain held Florida and a large stretch of land from Texas to California. New France worried the British most. The colony was smaller than the thirteen British colonies. Together with the expanse of French Louisiana, however, New France hemmed in the British along the coast.

The French and Native Americans

Another concern about the French was their relations with several Native American peoples. The French worked closely with Native Americans in the trade for animal skins and furs, offering better prices than the British. Also, the Native Americans knew that the British threatened their way of life. The French simply wanted control of the fur trade; British colonists wanted to settle on Indian land.

Growing Conflict

Throughout the 1700s, France and Britain fought several times in North America. In the late 1740s, the French felt threatened by the prospect of British settlement along the Ohio River, and so they built more forts in the region.

In 1754, Virginia **militia** and French forces clashed over Fort Duquesne, sited at present-day Pittsburgh. Originally built by the Ohio Company of Virginia, it was taken over by French forces. War seemed imminent.

Representatives from several colonies met at Albany, New York, in 1754. There, Benjamin Franklin proposed that the colonies form a union that could provide for their common defense. The **delegates** endorsed the plan, but the colonial governors later turned it down.

A Formidable Enemy

"These savages [Native Americans] may, indeed, be a formidable enemy to your raw American militia, but upon the King's regular and disciplined troops, sir, it is impossible they should make an impression."

General Edward Braddock to Benjamin Franklin, 1755

Braddock's Defeat

The British decided to take action against the French. In April 1755, General Edward Braddock led two regiments of 1,400 British troops from

The British recaptured Fort Duquesne in 1758. This picture shows a flag being raised at the fort that year, watched by George Washington (center, on horseback). Renamed Fort Pitt after the British prime minister, the site eventually became Pittsburgh.

Virginia to attack Fort Duquesne. He was joined by Virginia militia leader George Washington and 450 militiamen. Braddock foolishly led his soldiers into an ambush carried out by the French and their Indian allies. He was killed along with hundreds of his soldiers. Washington brought the survivors home.

The French and Indian War

The French and Indian War was now underway, although the British did not officially declare war until 1756. In 1756–1757, a French leader, Louis-Joseph, the Marquis de Montcalm, won several victories in upper New York. On July 1, 1758, his 3,000 men defeated a 12,000-strong British force at Fort Ticonderoga on the shores of Lake Champlain.

Later that month, however, British generals Jeffrey Amherst and James

British forces arrive on the Plains of Abraham to capture the French capital of Quebec in 1759.

Wolfe captured Louisbourg in Nova Scotia. The victory gave the British access to the St. Lawrence River, which meant they could strike deep into the heart of New France. That success was followed by the capture of Fort Duquesne.

British Victory at Quebec

The next summer, Wolfe led a large army to Quebec, the capital of New France. Other British forces captured Fort Niagara to the west and Fort Ticonderoga to the south. These victories prevented any reinforcements from reaching Montcalm at Quebec. The Battle of Quebec took place on September 12 and 13, 1759. British forces held the Plains of Abraham outside the city walls. Though out-numbered two to one, Montcalm attacked. The French met a thorough defeat in a battle that saw both Montcalm and Wolfe killed. A few days later, Quebec surrendered.

Conflicts between Britain and France continued for several more years, although most of the remaining fighting took place outside North America. In 1763, the Treaty of Paris ended the war, and France gave up all its holdings in North America either to Britain or to Spain, except for the city of New Orleans and two tiny islands near the St. Lawrence River.

Britain had largely eliminated its main rival from North America. But it would pay a high price for victory, both financially and by eventually losing the allegiance of its colonists.

First Steps to a New Conflict

Victory in the French and Indian War carried burdens for the British government. The ways Britain dealt with these burdens in the early 1760s caused resentment and tension to build in the thirteen colonies.

High Costs and New Territories

The first problem was that the French and Indian War had been costly, and Britain had been forced to borrow large sums of money to pay for it. Second, the British had to absorb the settlers of New France, now a British colony. New laws and systems were needed to rule them, and the government also faced the delicate task of bringing French-speaking, Catholic colonists into an English-speaking, Protestant-dominated empire.

Problems in the West

Third, Britain had to deal with white settlers and Native Americans in the **West**. Government officials feared that further attempts by British colonists to settle the West would inflame Native Americans, threaten trade with them, and lead to more fighting between colonists and Indian tribes.

Pontiac's War

The government's fears were confirmed early in 1763, just a few months after the Treaty of Paris was signed. On May 7, Native Americans in the Great Lakes region launched a widespread revolt.

The mastermind behind the rebellion was Pontiac, a chief of the Ottawa people. He had organized a loose alliance of Native peoples from Lake Superior to the lower Mississippi. The plan was simple: attack and seize every British fort on

Pontiac (c.1720–1769)

The son of an Ottawa father and a Chippewa mother, Pontiac was from the region around what is now Detroit, Michigan. He rose to the position of chief by his mid-thirties. He was influenced by Neolin, a Delaware Indian who preached that Native Americans needed to return to their traditional ways. Pontiac focused his own attention on an anti-British message. After the failure of his 1763 rebellion, however, he decided to ally himself with the British. Over time, however, Pontiac's power waned, in part because he acted arrogantly. In 1766, he killed a rival leader and was rejected by his people. A few years later, some historical accounts claim, Pontiac was himself murdered at Cahokia in present-day Illinois.

Ottawa chief Pontiac addresses a crowd of people, urging them to reject European culture.

the frontier in May 1763. Native Americans captured eight forts across the region, but two important forts— Fort Pitt (formerly Fort Duquesne) and Fort Detroit in Michigan—held out against attack.

Pontiac himself laid **siege** to Detroit, an effort that lasted several months. His Native American allies, however, were unwilling to sustain the effort, and he had to break off the siege. Still, it was 1766 before

Pontiac agreed to sign a peace treaty with the British.

The Proclamation of 1763

In the spring of 1763, the British had begun discussing the idea of limiting western settlement. Pontiac's Rebellion, as it became known, convinced them this was a necessary course. So on October 7, 1763, King George III signed the Proclamation of 1763. The chief parts of this decree were simple and straightforward:

- British colonists were forbidden from settling lands west of the Appalachian Mountains.

- Any settlers who were already there had to leave.
- Any trade with Indians would be carried out by British officials, not by Americans.

Colonists talked about being denied their rights to live where they wished. They uttered angry words about British high-handedness, and they ignored the proclamation by continuing to stream west.

A Permanent Army

Pontiac's Rebellion and worries over future problems between whites and Native Americans convinced the British to position soldiers permanently in North America. Given the large expanse of territory, they would need a lot of troops.

How to pay for these troops was a major question. By early 1763, the British government owed huge sums of money. Taxes in Britain had been high throughout the war, and many people there resented paying taxes to fund colonial expenses.

Solving the Financial Crisis

Facing this problem was George Grenville, who was both prime minister and

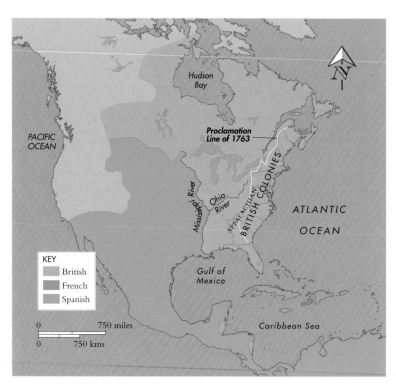

The Proclamation Line of 1763 limited white settlement to east of the Appalachian Mountains, even though the land to the west was now British. This law caused resentment for years to come.

Native Americans launched attacks on colonists' homes in the West to try to drive away the new settlers. In an attempt to control the situation, Britain sent soldiers to the region to defend the colonists. The colonists wanted protection, but they did not want to pay for it through taxes imposed in Britain.

Chancellor of the Exchequer (the chief minister of the British treasury) in 1763. Grenville did not really believe the colonies should pay the massive debt the British government owed. The cost of stationing soldiers in North America, however, was another matter. Those soldiers, after all, were protecting the colonists from possible Native American attacks. The high expense of keeping an army in America seemed an unfair burden for taxpayers in Britain.

Grenville's Plan

Since 1733, the colonists had faced a tax of 6 pennies per gallon on molasses imported to North America on foreign-owned ships. The colonists had always been reluctant to pay taxes and avoided them if possible. Tax collection in the colonies was not strictly enforced. The Molasses Act taxes had just been ignored—American merchants simply bribed **customs** officials to look the other way when they brought in molasses. Knowing

No Enforcement

"It was a matter of astonishment to observe what little care was taken to enforce the laws. . . . The merchants . . . had commonly undertaken those voyages which afforded the greatest prospect of gain, without any further regard to their illegality than, that the [customs officials] must be silenced, and, by what means was but too obvious."

British Board of Trade, "Observations on the Trade and Revenue of North America," 1763

this, Grenville came up with a plan to raise money from the tax to pay for at least some of the military expenses. He proposed halving the tax to just 3 pennies per gallon, but the catch was that he planned on having the tax actually collected.

The Sugar Act

Grenville believed that, since he was lowering the molasses tax, Americans would now be willing to pay it. On April 5, 1764, Parliament passed the American Revenue Act, commonly known as the Sugar Act. Along with lowering the tax rate on foreign molasses, the new law raised the tax on foreign refined sugar and raised or introduced new taxes on other non-British goods. It also banned the import of foreign rum or French wines into the colonies. In addition, the Sugar Act created new regulations for enforcing the law and set out harsh punishments for anyone found breaking it.

For the first time, Parliament had created a tax in the colonies aimed at raising revenue to fund government activities. Grenville also appointed new tax collectors, men who would

The Proclamation and the French Canadians

The inhabitants of the former New France, now part of British Canada, were no more pleased about the Proclamation of 1763 than other British colonists. The decree made them subject to British law, and the French Canadians worried about this provision. In the first place, they were accustomed to the French legal system, which worked differently. Further, British law had several anti-Catholic features that would limit French Canadians' rights.

A woman in the Carolinas beats back an official who has come to claim taxes.

not accept bribes. The Royal Navy began cruising off the American coast to stop any ships guilty of smuggling.

The Colonists' Response

The colonists quickly viewed the new law with anger. The assemblies of nine colonies sent messages to Parliament protesting it. Most protested at first about the economic impact, arguing that the law would reduce trade.

Some, however, said it was a matter of rights. Massachusetts lawyer James Otis drafted a message saying the tax "deprive[d] the colonies of some of their most essential rights as British subjects, and . . . particularly the right of assessing their own taxes."

CHAPTER FIVE

Clashes in the Colonies

The tax issue arose once again in 1765. Grenville persuaded Parliament to pass the Stamp Act, putting a tax on a wide range of goods, including printed matter (books, newspapers, and pamphlets), legal documents, and ships' cargo lists; and playing cards and dice.

Introducing the Stamp Act

To British members of Parliament, the tax seemed perfectly reasonable. A similar tax had been in effect in Britain since 1694. When the idea was suggested in early 1764, however, colonial agents and other Americans in Britain had warned the government against it.

Despite the warnings, Grenville proposed the tax. On March 22, 1765, Parliament approved it by nearly a four-to-one margin. Grenville named important colonists as agents, or collectors of the tax, hoping this would show the colonists that their leading citizens accepted the law.

The Assemblies Protest

The colonists, however, protested hotly over the issue of taxation. Since the colonists had no elected representative in Parliament, they said, the government had no authority to tax them. "Taxation without representaton," they declared, denied them their rights as British citizens.

Virginia's assembly, the House of Burgesses, met at the end of May 1765. A newly elected member, Patrick Henry, introduced several **resolutions** that the Burgesses approved. Word spread through the colonies that the Virginia Resolves were a defiant assertion of American rights. By year's end, the assemblies of eight

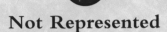

colonies approved resolutions declaring that Parliament had no right to tax the colonies in order to raise revenue.

The organization for the colonists' protests came from Massachusetts. In June 1765, the Massachusetts assembly issued a letter to the other colonial assemblies asking them to send delegates to a meeting about the Stamp

After the Stamp Act of 1765, stamps such as these (above and below left) were attached to goods to show how much tax was due. Anyone selling taxed goods was obliged to use the stamps.

Act. That October, representatives came from nine of the thirteen colonies to the Stamp Act Congress in New York City. They asked Parliament to **repeal** the hated Stamp Act and declared that only colonial legislatures could enact taxes.

In mid-August, meanwhile, the Sons of Liberty, a group of anti-tax protestors, burned an **effigy** of a tax collector in Boston. A few days later, protestors attacked the homes of other British officials. Across the colonies, stamp agents were threatened with harm if they actually tried to issue stamps. Merchants in New York City signed a nonimportation agreement, in which they pledged not to import

The Sons of Liberty

Outside of the colonial assemblies, much of the protest against the Stamp Act was organized by the Sons of Liberty, a group formed in Boston in 1765. Although supported by several political leaders, the group comprised mostly tradesmen and several printers and publishers, all greatly affected by the Stamp Act. By the end of 1765, Sons of Liberty groups existed in all the colonies, where they organized acts of **sabotage** and sometimes violent protests. As news of their actions spread widely through newspapers and pamphlets, the movement grew rapidly. The Sons of Liberty became a vital part of the effort to resist British control and unite the colonies.

The commissioner of customs in Boston was hung out of his window to be covered in hot tar and stuck with feathers. The Sons of Liberty often used "tarring and feathering" as a punishment for tax collectors and other government officials.

No Money

"The avenues of trade are all shut up. We have no remittances and are at our wits' end for want of money to fulfill our engagements with our tradesmen."

Merchant from Bristol, England, complaining to Parliament about the impact of the nonimportation agreements, 1766

any goods from Britain as long as the Stamp Act remained in force. Those in other colonies soon followed suit. The colonists had found a way to put economic pressure on Britain.

Repeal of the Stamp Act

All the turmoil disturbed the British. Grenville had been removed from office, and the new prime minister, Charles, Lord Rockingham, opposed the Stamp Act and would have been happy to see it repealed. Many

This cartoon was published in 1766, when the Stamp Act was repealed. It shows a funeral for "Miss Ame-Stamp" at a quay in London where goods were loaded on ships. On the right is a large container of unused "Stamps from America."

members of Parliament, however, were angry about the colonists' defi-ance. On the other hand, British merchants were suffering from the nonimportation agreements. Stressing this problem, Rockingham convinced Parliament to repeal the hated Stamp Act in March 1766. The colonists rejoiced, having won a great victory. But news of the repeal of the Stamp Act was accompanied by news of another law Parliament had passed. In the Declaratory Act of March 1766, Parliament threw down a clear challenge to the colonists. Parliament, the law said, had the "full power and authority to make laws . . . to bind the colonies and people of America . . . in all cases whatsoever."

New Leader, New Plan

By July 1776, Rockingham had lost the support he needed to remain in office. The new prime minister was

Disgrace

"William Jackson, an importer . . . : It is desired that the Sons and Daughters of Liberty would not buy any one thing of him, for in so doing they will bring disgrace upon themselves and their posterity, for ever and ever, Amen."

Boston broadside, displayed to discourage people from doing business with a merchant who did not sign nonimportation agreements, 1770

Much to the irritation of colonists, British soldiers, sent from England to keep order, march through the streets of Boston.

William Pitt, a supporter of the colonists who had led the British government during the French and Indian War. Pitt was aging and ill, however, and Chancellor of the Exchequer Charles Townshend in effect led the government.

Townshend proposed a new tax plan in May 1767, and Parliament approved it the next month. The plan put duties on several different products, including glass, lead, paints, paper, and tea. Once more, protests swept across the colonies, and again merchants signed nonimportation pledges against Britain.

Tempers were sharper this time. In Massachusetts in 1768, political leader Samuel Adams persuaded the assembly to issue a letter to other colonies asking them to protest the tax and to

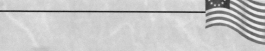

Putting up the Troops

Another issue dividing the government and the colonists was the Quartering Act. This 1765 law required the colonial assemblies to provide barracks for British soldiers in North America and to furnish them with food. The colonial assemblies were torn. If they ignored the law, they were in defiance. Some avoided the issue by providing a little of what was needed. This reluctance cost the colonists some support in Britain. Even those who sympathized with the cause found it hard to accept the colonists' refusal to help British soldiers.

Boston engraver Paul Revere produced and circulated this engraving of the Boston Massacre. The image encouraged colonists to believe that the British were willing to kill innocent Americans.

discuss joint action against it. In response, Massachusetts governor Francis Bernard simply shut down the Massachusetts assembly, using his authority to take away its powers.

The *Liberty* Incident

Customs officials in Boston, meanwhile, had worries of their own. They were being harassed by Boston's citizens and blocked from collecting taxes. In June 1768, one customs officer boarded the ship *Liberty,* owned by merchant John Hancock, to collect the required tax on imported wine. The crew simply locked the official in a cabin while they unloaded the goods. Tax officials later seized Hancock's ship, but their action brought such violent protests that they had to flee for safety. British officials asked the army to send more troops to Boston to protect them.

The Boston Massacre

By 1769, British trade with the colonies had fallen dramatically. The government realized it might need to repeal the Townshend Acts. Before it could do so, however, violence erupted. All during the winter, the presence of British troops in Boston had

The Boston State House, where the Massachusetts assembly met, was built in 1713 and is the oldest surviving public building in the city. The stone circle in the foreground marks the site of the Boston Massacre.

angered colonists in the city. Crowds jeered at the soldiers, and children pelted them with rocks. On March 5, 1770, an unruly crowd gathered near some soldiers led by Captain Thomas Preston. In the face of insults and thrown objects, the soldiers fired a volley into the crowd. Three people were killed instantly; several more were wounded, two of whom died soon after.

Hundreds of colonists roamed the streets, looking for vengeance. Samuel Adams forcibly persuaded the new Massachusetts royal governor, Thomas Hutchinson, to pull all troops out of the city to avoid further bloodshed. That action—along with the arrest of Captain Preston and eight of his soldiers—calmed the situation.

The Tax Issue

Yet another new prime minister, Frederick, Lord North, had been working in 1770 to withdraw all the hated Townshend taxes except the one on tea, kept as a symbol of British authority. The approval for the repeal came in April 1770, just a few weeks after the Boston Massacre.

At a meeting in Boston, a crowd voted to keep the nonimportation agreements in effect as long as the tea tax remained. Other colonies then did the same. The colonies as well as Britain were suffering from the lack of trade, however, and soon the non-

importation agreements weakened. Merchants in New York City were the first to start importing goods again, and other colonies followed suit.

Outrageous Mob

"So far was I from intending the death of any person that I suffered the troops to go to the spot where the unhappy affair took place without any loading in their [guns]; nor did I ever give orders for loading them. . . . [But] the mob still increased and were more outrageous, striking their clubs and bludgeons one against another, and calling out, 'Come on you rascals, . . . fire if you dare.'"

Captain Thomas Preston, giving his account of the Boston Massacre, 1770

The Soldiers' Trial

John Adams—a cousin of Samuel Adams and an up-and-coming young lawyer—defended Captain Thomas Preston and his eight soldiers when they were brought to trial in 1770. Although he was a firm supporter of the protests, Adams believed that everyone deserved a fair trial. He was able to show there was no proof that Preston had ordered the troops to fire, and Preston was acquitted of murder charges. Adams also stoutly defended the soldiers, arguing that the mob's behavior had been extreme and no doubt incited the soldiers to act. The jury apparently agreed. It acquitted the soldiers of murder, although two were found guilty of manslaughter.

CHAPTER SIX

The Fuse Burns

From 1770 to 1772, the situation in America calmed down. Since Parliament passed no new taxes, there were no new issues to fight. The taxes on tea and molasses remained, and merchants paid them, although some continued to smuggle. The lack of turmoil and renewal of trade helped revive the colonies' economies, which in turn promoted greater calm. The British even allowed the Massachusetts legislature to reassemble.

The *Gaspée* Incident

In 1772, tension increased once again. British customs officers—still unwilling to be bribed—vigorously pursued ships looking for illegal goods. Some patrolled the waters off Rhode Island in the *Gaspée*, and colonists resented the ship's presence. When the *Gaspée* accidentally ran aground in June, a crowd of protestors swarmed toward it, seized the crew, and burned the ship.

More Trouble in Boston

Back in Boston, more trouble was brewing. Just a few days after the *Gaspée* burned, Massachusetts

Restraint of Liberty

"There must be an abridgment of what are called English liberties. . . . I wish the good of the colony when I wish to see some further restraint of liberty rather than the connection with the parent state should be broken."

Massachusetts governor Thomas Hutchinson, letter to British minister Thomas Whately, written between 1767 and 1769

Samuel Adams (1722–1803)

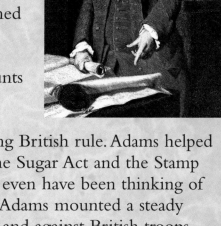

A leader of Boston protests, Samuel Adams was a superb political organizer. Little in his early life would have predicted this talent. After graduating from Harvard College, Adams briefly tried the law but abandoned that career. He then proved a failure in business. Adams served as a tax collector from 1756 to 1764, but he left his accounts in terrible shape.

By 1764, however, he had found his calling in politics and his cause in fighting British rule. Adams helped lead Boston's vigorous protests against the Sugar Act and the Stamp Act. As early as the late 1760s, he might even have been thinking of independence as the colonists' real goal. Adams mounted a steady campaign against Governor Hutchinson and against British troops stationed in Boston. When tempers calmed after the repeal of the Townshend Acts, Adams kept working against the British.

Adams later served in the Continental Congress, but he was more of a force back in Massachusetts. After the Revolution, he became lieutenant governor and governor of Massachusetts before retiring.

royal governor Thomas Hutchinson informed the colonial assembly that it no longer needed to pay his salary. Instead, he announced, he would be paid by the British Crown. Judges in Massachusetts, Hutchinson added, would also be paid by Britain.

The delegates and other colonists smelled danger: officials paid by the king, they believed, could easily be swayed by the king. Suspicion of this new arrangement increased in 1773, when letters that Hutchinson had written some years earlier surfaced. In the letters, he had urged the British to clamp down on the protestors. Colonists' rights, he said, were less important than order.

The committees of correspondence promoted unity through their letters by sharing information and organizing meetings. This cartoon, first published by Benjamin Franklin in 1754, came to symbolize the growing movement among the colonies for unity.

Committees of Correspondence

The *Gaspée* incident and the controversy over Hutchinson's salary and letters stirred opposition once again. In November 1772, Samuel Adams organized a town meeting in Boston. He convinced the crowd to form a committee of correspondence whose job would be to communicate with other towns and so promote unity in the struggle for rights. Adams wrote the first communication himself, a harsh criticism of British actions and a clear explanation of how those actions took away the colonists' rights. By mid-1773, committees of correspondence had formed in other colonies.

The East India Company

The year 1773 saw new problems. Decades earlier, the British had formed the British East India Company, which exported tea from India. In the early 1770s, the company was in danger of going out of business,

and Lord North decided to allow the company to sell tea directly to American merchants. In the past, the company sold tea to British wholesalers, who sold it to American wholesalers, who in turn sold it to American merchants. By eliminating the two intermediate steps with the Tea Act of May 1773, North made it possible for the company to earn more for selling its tea. At the same time, the price of tea would drop since it would go through fewer hands. Of course, American wholesalers would suffer, but Lord North undoubtedly assumed that lower tea prices would seem more important to the colonists.

He was, as British officials so often were in the 1760s and 1770s, mistaken. The colonists saw the Tea Act as a threat. The deal would give the East India Company a controlling share of the tea market, making it possible to raise prices whenever it wished. The colonists decided not to buy tea.

Daughters of Liberty

Women played a vital role in the nonimportation movement, since they carried out household purchases and could be the ones to **boycott** British products such as sugar, tea, paper, and fabrics. Many women, calling themselves the Daughters of Liberty, signed their own nonimportation agreements to signal their support for the cause. More than fifty women of Edenton, North Carolina, issued a statement saying it was their right and duty to join in this effort. This action was very unusual because women in the eighteenth century were considered to be without any political rights at all. Like others all over the colonies, the women of Edenton spun and wove their own cloth and made tea from local herbs and other plants instead of buying it.

A British cartoon depicts the women of Edenton in action against British taxes.

The Sons of Liberty who took part in the Boston Tea Party dressed as Indians when they boarded the tea ships to throw the cargo overboard.

The Boston Tea Party

The East India company dispatched tea-filled ships to America, but when colonists refused to buy the tea, many ship captains sailed back to Britain. In Boston, however, Governor Hutchinson ordered the ships to dock and prepare to unload their cargoes of tea.

On the night of December 16, 1773, a group of Bostonian Sons of Liberty boarded the ships and tossed more than 340 cases of tea into the harbor. When news spread of the "Boston Tea Party," some colonists in New York City dumped tea from British Ships into their own harbor.

The Intolerable Acts

The British were not amused. Parliament met in the spring of 1774 and passed several new laws aimed at punishing the colonies—especially Massachusetts:

- The Boston Port Bill closed the port of Boston to trade ships.

Privileges Denied

"Every privilege you [Americans] at present claim as a birthright, may be wrested from you by the same authority that blockades the town of Boston."

Anonymous Georgian,
reacting to the Intolerable Acts, 1774

The King's Response

"Concessions have made matters worse. The time has come for compulsion."

King George III, responding
to the Boston Tea Party, 1774

- The Administration of Justice Act protected British officials from being sued by colonists.
- The Massachusetts Regulating Act put much of Massachusetts under control of the Crown.
- A new Quartering Act said colonists had to house British soldiers if requested to do so.
- The Quebec Act set up new rules for governing Canada that increased government powers and extended the territory of Canada down to the Ohio River.

Parliament called the first four of these laws the Coercive Acts because it wanted to coerce, or force, the colonies to submit to British law. The colonists named all five laws "the Intolerable Acts."

Protest in Virginia

Virginia's House of Burgesses declared June 1, 1774—the day the port of Boston would be closed—as a day of fasting and prayer. This act of support was quickly punished by Virginia's governor, who shut down the House of Burgesses. The members responded by meeting illegally in a tavern. They passed a resolution urging all colonies to send delegates to a meeting to talk about what to do.

The First Congress and the Suffolk Resolves

That meeting—the First Continental Congress—began September 5, 1774, in Philadelphia. Fifty-six delegates, coming from all the colonies except Georgia, showed up.

Meanwhile, a group of colonists met near Boston and approved a set of resolutions called the Suffolk Resolves. These resolutions blasted the Intolerable Acts as illegal because they violated the British constitution. They urged the people of Massachusetts to form a government of their own. They called for renewed economic action against British imports. Finally, they said colonists should begin military training.

A minister offers a prayer at the opening of the First Continental Congress at Carpenters' Hall, Philadelphia, in September 1775. The meeting was attended by such colonial leaders as Samuel Adams, John Adams, and Patrick Henry.

Paul Revere traveled on horseback to carry the Suffolk Resolves to the Congress in Philadelphia, where the document was approved on September 17. Next, the Congress approved a declaration of colonists' rights and liberties. Then it called for a complete shutdown of all trade—both imports and exports—with Britain. The Congress prepared an address, covering these points, to the king and the people of Britain.

Declaration and Resolves

"The foundation of English liberty, and of all free government, is a right in the people to participate in their legislative council: and as the English colonists are not represented, . . .
in the British Parliament, they are entitled to a free and exclusive power of legislation in their several provincial legislatures, where their right of representation can alone be preserved.
. . .We cheerfully consent to the operation of such Acts of the British Parliament, . . . excluding every idea of taxation, internal or external, for raising a revenue on the subjects of America without their consent."

First Continental Congress, Declaration and Resolves, October 14, 1774

A Challenge

The messages were mostly polite, but they were a challenge to the British king and Parliament. Taking a stand of this kind was unheard of in the 1770s, when people were supposed to be loyal and obedient to their rulers. The British would have the chance to respond, but the colonists would then decide if that response was acceptable. The delegates agreed to meet again in spring 1775 to discuss whether their grievances had been addressed and decide what to do next.

Nearly a quarter century had passed since 1750. Great changes had taken place in the relations between the colonists and Britain. In the next few years, even more startling changes would occur.

Carpenters' Hall (below) was the meeting place for the delegates who attended the First Continental Congress. The building still stands in Philadelphia today.

Time Line

1754   Virginia militia clash with French forces in present-day Ohio.
Delegates of several colonies meet at Albany Congress.

1755   British forces under General Edward Braddock are defeated by French soldiers and Native Americans near Fort Duquesne, launching French and Indian War.

1756   French commander Marquis de Montcalm wins first in series of victories against the British.

1758   British capture Louisbourg.

1759   British capture Quebec.

1760   George III becomes king of Britain.

1763   February 10: Treaty of Paris ends French and Indian War.
May 7: Native Americans under Pontiac launch revolt against British rule.
October 7: Britain issues Proclamation of 1763.

1764   April 5: Parliament passes Sugar Act to raise money to defend colonies.

1765   Sons of Liberty forms in Boston.
March 22: Parliament passes Stamp Act, causing widespread protests in colonies.
May 29: Virginia's House of Burgesses passes Virginia Resolves, asserting colonists' rights.

October 7–25: Colonists meet in Stamp Act Congress.

1766   March 18: Stamp Act is repealed; Parliament passes Declaratory Act.

1767   June 29: Parliament passes Townshend Acts, creating new taxes.

1768   June 10: British officials in Boston seize the *Liberty* for smuggling.

1770   March 5: Boston Massacre.
April: Townshend Acts are repealed.

1772   June 9: Revenue ship *Gaspée* is burned in Rhode Island.
November 2: Boston town meeting appoints first committee of correspondence.

1773   May 10: Tea Act goes into effect.
December 16: Colonists in Boston destroy more than 340 casks of tea in Boston Tea Party.

1774   March 31: Parliament passes first of Coercive Acts (also known as "Intolerable Acts").
September 5–26: First Continental Congress meets in Philadelphia and issues address to the British government defending colonists' rights.

1776   British colonies in North America declare independence from Britain.

1781   Britain surrenders to Patriot forces at Yorktown, Virginia.

1783   Britain recognizes U.S. independence.

Glossary

boycott: refuse to do business with a particular company or country in protest of its policies.

cash crops: crops grown to be sold rather than for farmers' own consumption.

colony: settlement, area, or country owned or controlled by another nation.

congress: meeting. The name "Congress" was given to the first meetings of delegates from the British colonies and was then adopted as the name of the U.S. legislature when the United States formed a national government.

constitution: document that lays down the basic rules and laws of a nation or organization.

customs: government body that collects duties or taxes due on imports and exports.

delegate: person chosen to represent a group at a meeting or in making decisions.

economic: having to do with the economy, which is the system of producing and distributing goods and services.

effigy: image or figure representing a person who is disliked.

empire: political power that controls large territory of colonies or other nations.

Enlightenment: intellectual movement of the 1600s and 1700s that valued reason, individual liberties, and the people's right to determine their own form of government.

legislature: group of officials that makes laws.

militia: group of citizens organized into an army (as opposed to an army of professional soldiers, or regulars).

monarch: king, queen, or emperor—person who rules a kingdom or an empire. Monarchs are not elected, and their roles vary from that of absolute ruler to just honorary head of state.

Puritan: person belonging to a Protestant Christian group that wanted to purify the Church of England.

Quaker: member of the Society of Friends, a Christian group that has no ministers or rituals and opposes all war and violence.

repeal: undo an earlier decision or law.

republic: nation that is led by elected officials and that has no monarch.

resolution: statement of principle by a legislative assembly.

sabotage: destruction or other hurtful act intended to cause problems for an enemy.

siege: military operation in which a group of attackers surrounds a target and either attacks it or keeps it trapped in an attempt to force it to surrender.

smuggle: illegally bring goods into a place.

tax: sum charged by the government on purchases, property ownership, or income and used to pay for public services or the cost of governing.

West: area of North America in the 1700s and early 1800s between the original thirteen colonies and the Mississippi River.

Further Resources

Books

Hakim, Joy. *Making Thirteen Colonies* (A History of US volume 1). Oxford University Press, 2002.

Knight, James E. *Boston Tea Party: Rebellion in the Colonies* (Adventures in Colonial America). Troll, 1998.

Lukes, Bonnie L. *The Boston Massacre* (Famous Trials). Lucent, 1998.

Quackenbush, Robert. *Daughter of Liberty: A True Story of the American Revolution.* Hyperion, 1999.

Steins, Richard. *Colonial America* (The Making of America). Raintree, 2000.

Places to Visit

Boston National Historic Park
Charlestown Navy Yard
Boston, MA 02129
Telephone: (617) 242-5642

Web Sites

Boston National Historic Park
www.nps.gov/bost/
National Park Service site has information on events and places in Boston, including the Boston Massacre site and Paul Revere's House. "In Depth" link offers a virtual tour of Boston's historic Freedom Trail.

The British Empire
www.britishempire.co.uk/
Web site devoted to the history of the British Empire.

Colonial America 1600–1775
falcon.jmu.edu/~ramseyil/colonial.htm
Web site offers links to and descriptions of many resources on colonial America, ranging from primary-source documents and maps to information about plantations and everyday life.

The Seven Years War Website (French and Indian War)
www.militaryheritage.com/7yrswar.htm
Web site with articles, images, video clips, and sound clips to do with the French and Indian War.

Index